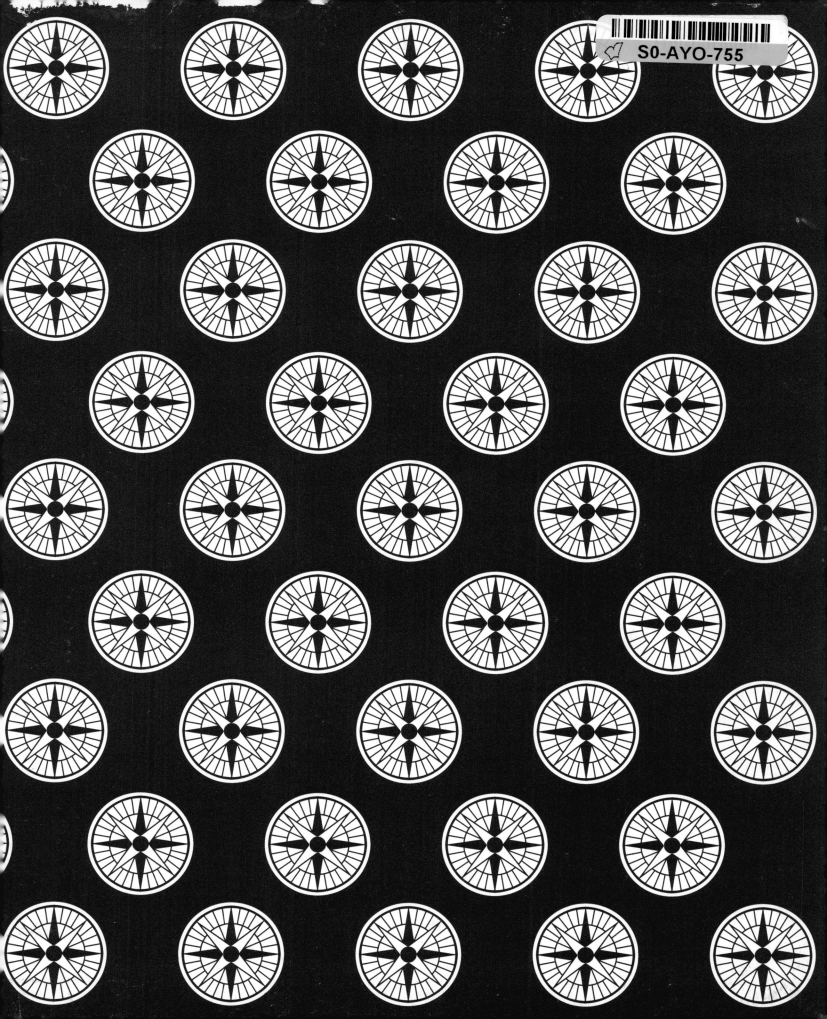

I Wonder Why

Columbus Crossed The Ocean

and Other Questions About Explorers

Rosie Greenwood

KINGFISHER

BOSTON

KINGFISHER
a Houghton Mifflin Company imprint
222 Berkeley Street
Boston, Massachusetts 02116
www.houghtonmifflinbooks.com

First published in 2005
10 9 8 7 6 5 4 3 2 1

1TR/0305/SHE/RNB(RNB)/126.6MA/F

LIBRARY OF CONGRESS CATALOGING-IN-PUBLICATION DATA
Greenwood, Rosie.
I wonder why Columbus crossed the ocean and
   other questions about explorers/Rosie
   Greenwood.—1st ed.
             p. cm.
Includes index.
1. Discoveries in geography—Miscellanea—Juvenile
   literature. 2. Explorers—Miscellanea—Juvenile
   literature. I. Title.
G175.G734   2005
910'.92'2—dc22   2004028265

ISBN 0-7534-5860-8
ISBN 978-07534-5860-0

Series designer: David West Children's Books
Author: Rosie Greenwood
Illustrations: Marrion Appleton 8tl; Chris Forsey 8t, 10–11;
Richard Hook 12–13, 22–23c; John
James 6bl, 17tr; Peter Jones (John
Martin) 14–15m; Mike Lacey
16–17, 18–19, 22l, 23r; Linden
Artists 5br; Mortlemans/Phillips
19; Alex Pang 8br; Neil Reed
24–25c, 30t; Bernard Robinson
4–5m; John Spires 12tr;
Ross Watton front cover;
Mike White 9b, 19b, 23br,
25b, 26; Paul Wright 17br,
20–21c; Peter Wilkes
(SGA) all cartoons.

Printed in Taiwan

CONTENTS

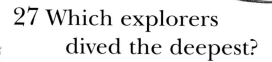

Who were the first explorers?

Some of the earliest ocean voyages were made by the Polynesian peoples of New Guinea. As long as 3,500 years ago they began leaving their homeland to explore the vast Pacific Ocean in boats no bigger than canoes.

● Over hundreds of years different groups of Polynesians settled on thousands of Pacific islands.

Where was Punt?

As people sailed off in canoes from New Guinea, thousands of miles away in Egypt much larger trading ships were sent to the land of Punt. This was many miles south of Egypt at the tip of the Red Sea. Punt was discovered by Egyptian explorers in ancient times.

● Around 2,300 years ago the Greek explorer Pytheas sailed north past Spain, France, and Great Britain. He may have even reached Norway.

Who was Hanno?

One thousand years later Hanno set sail from the trading city of Carthage on what is today the coast of Tunisia. Hanno was one of the first known explorers.

● Hanno's ships sailed west into the Atlantic Ocean and then south, staying close to the African coast. They may have sailed as far as the country we now call Sierra Leone.

Why did people go exploring?

Over hundreds of years explorers have had all types of reasons for taking off on their travels. Some were looking for new lands to trade with or to settle in and farm. Others wanted to spread word of their religion. Some hoped to achieve fame or riches, and many simply set off in search of adventures.

Northwest Passage

CANADA

Rocky Mountains

NORTH AMERICA

Gulf of St. Lawrence

ATLANTIC OCEAN

Tenochtitlán

WEST INDIES

Galapagos Islands

SOUTH AMERICA

● In around the year A.D. 1000 a daring band of Viking explorers led by Leif Eriksson became the first Europeans to sail across the Atlantic Ocean to North America.

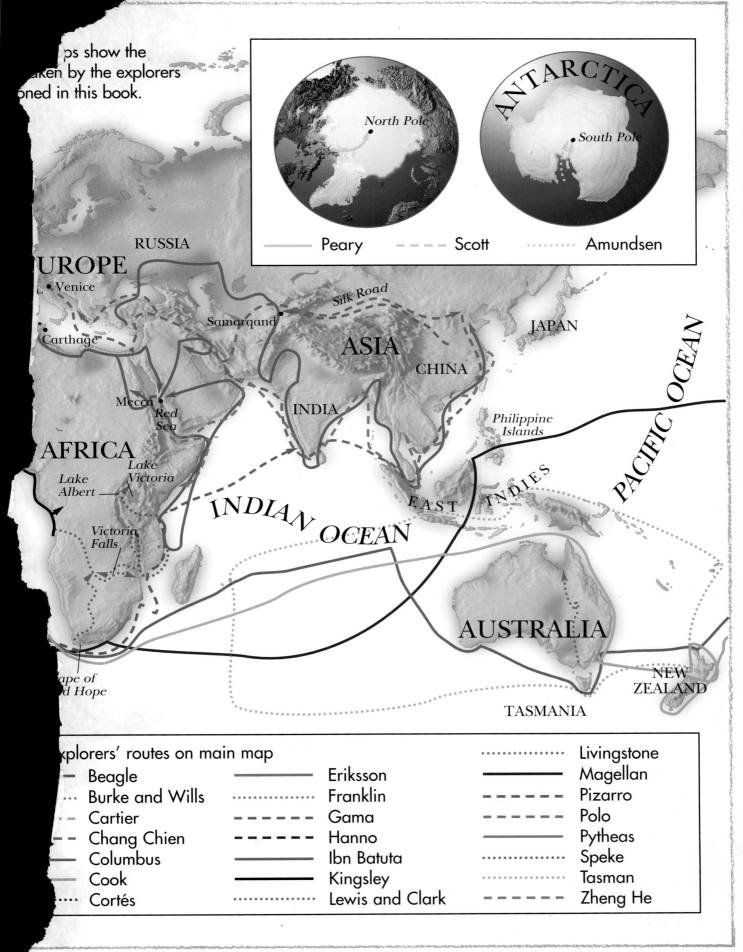

...ps show the
...ken by the explorers
...oned in this book.

North Pole

ANTARCTICA

South Pole

——— Peary   – – – Scott   ·········· Amundsen

RUSSIA

...UROPE

• Venice

Carthage

Silk Road

Samarqand

JAPAN

ASIA

CHINA

Mecca •
*Red
Sea*

INDIA

Philippine
Islands

PACIFIC OCEAN

AFRICA

*Lake
Victoria*

*Lake
Albert*

INDIAN OCEAN

EAST INDIES

*Victoria
Falls*

AUSTRALIA

NEW
ZEALAND

...ape of
...d Hope

TASMANIA

...xplorers' routes on main map

– Beagle
···· Burke and Wills
– · Cartier
– – Chang Chien
——— Columbus
——— Cook
····· Cortés

——— Eriksson
·········· Franklin
– – – – Gama
– – – Hanno
——— Ibn Batuta
——— Kingsley
·········· Lewis and Clark

·········· Livingstone
——— Magellan
– – – Pizarro
– – – Polo
——— Pytheas
·········· Speke
·········· Tasman
– – – – Zheng He

What made early explorers starstruck?

The first explorers did not have compasses to help them find their way. Instead they learned to use the position of the stars in the night sky in order to guide them. The Sun's position helped them during the day.

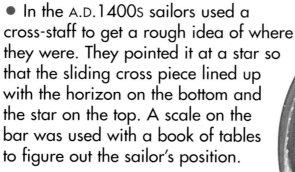

● In the A.D. 1400s sailors used a cross-staff to get a rough idea of where they were. They pointed it at a star so that the sliding cross piece lined up with the horizon on the bottom and the star on the top. A scale on the bar was used with a book of tables to figure out the sailor's position.

● The compass was invented in China—Chinese sailors were using it to help them find their way more than 1,000 years ago.

- These m
routes t▢
menti▢

- Early explorers figured out how fast they were traveling by timing how long it took a floating object to travel their ship's length.

OCEANUS
EUROPA
MEDITERRANEAN SEA
AFRICA
ASIA

F▢y did explorers ▢en get lost?

▢nt maps were mostly guesswork
▢se people knew so little about the
▢. World maps didn't begin to improve
▢l the A.D. 1500s, when explorers made
▢first round-the-world voyages.

- For hundreds of years Europeans based their maps on this one, drawn by the Greek scholar Ptolemy in the A.D. 100s.

PORTUG▢
SPAIN

SIERRA
LEONE

C▢
Goo

Key to e▢

When did the East discover the West?

In 127 B.C. after a long and very dangerous journey, a traveler named Chang Chien reached Samarqand in central Asia. He was the first known Chinese explorer to journey outside of China, and the first to learn about the great civilizations of the West such as ancient Rome.

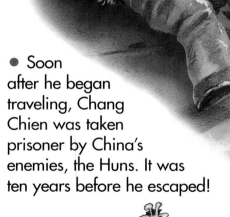

● Soon after he began traveling, Chang Chien was taken prisoner by China's enemies, the Huns. It was ten years before he escaped!

Who set sail in junks?

Chinese explorers did—junks are Chinese sailing ships. One of the greatest Chinese explorers was named Zheng He. By Zheng He's time—the early A.D. 1400s—Chinese junks dwarfed European ships.

● Zheng He's fleet of junks sailed as far as east Africa and brought home a giraffe!

Whose journey lasted 24 years?

The Arab explorer Ibn Batuta's adventures began in A.D. 1325, when he set out from his hometown of Tangier in Morocco. He was bitten by the travel bug so hard that he didn't return home again until 1349!

● Ibn Batuta wrote a book about his travels, but his memory wasn't always very good. He said that he had seen hippos with horselike heads and that the pyramids were cone shaped!

What was the Silk Road?

In the centuries following Chang Chien's journey to central Asia, traders began using his route to carry all types of luxury goods between China and Europe. Europeans named it the Silk Road because silk was at the top of their list of Chinese luxuries.

● Silk thread comes from the cocoons of caterpillars that munch away on mulberry leaves.

● For hundreds of years no one outside of China knew how silk was made. The punishment for giving away the secret was death.

● Then in the A.D. 550s the Roman emperor sent two monks to China as spies. Cleverly, they hid caterpillar eggs in their walking sticks and managed to smuggle them out of China—the secret was out!

Which Italian teenager traveled the Silk Road?

Marco Polo was only 17 years old in A.D. 1271, when he set out from Venice with his father and uncle. The three travelers sailed to the Middle East. Then they traveled overland, becoming the first known Europeans to make it to the Silk Road's end in China.

● No one knows when the Italians first made ice cream, but Marco Polo may have brought a recipe for water ices back with him from China.

Why did Columbus cross the ocean?

When the great Italian-born explorer Christopher Columbus set sail from Spain in 1492, he was hoping to find a western sea route to China. He hoped that sailing there would be quicker and safer than traveling overland along the Silk Road.

● Like other Europeans of his time, Columbus had no idea that the Americas and the islands of the West Indies lay between him and China.

Did he find what he was looking for?

Columbus never found his western sea route. Nor did he know that he had reached the Americas. He always believed that the West Indies, where he first landed, was part of Asia.

• The first European to sail to India was Portugal's Vasco da Gama in 1497–1498. Unlike Columbus, he headed south around Africa and then east, not west.

What was life like on board?

Ordinary sailors ate and slept on the bare boards of the ship's deck—they had no tables and no beds. A sailor's life was hard work, with few comforts of home.

• Things improved after Columbus' men got to the West Indies and noticed the local people sleeping in hanging beds. The European name for this useful invention was the hammock.

Who were the conquistadores?

In Europe people soon realized that Columbus had stumbled across the Americas. Rumors spread that they were rich in gold, and Spanish soldiers began traveling there in search of their fortunes. The soldiers were known as conquistadores, from the Spanish word for "conqueror," because they were more interested in conquering new lands than in exploring them.

● Unlike Europeans, the native peoples of the Americas didn't use gold as money. Instead they valued it for its beauty.

● The conquistadores were among the first Europeans to try the tasty things that until then were only grown in South America—from pineapples, tomatoes, and potatoes to chocolate.

Where was the city on a lake?

The beautiful city on a lake was Tenochtitlán—the capital of the Aztec people's vast empire in modern-day Mexico. The conquistador Hernán Cortés was the first European to see Tenochtitlán. His army invaded and conquered the Aztecs' lands in 1519–1521.

● Tenochtitlán was built on islands in Lake Texcoco. Like the Italian city of Venice, it was crisscrossed by canals and streets.

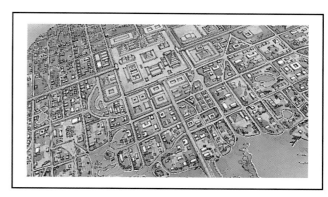

● In the A.D. 1530s conquistadores led by Francisco Pizarro conquered the huge empire of the Incas in the country that is now Peru.

Where was New France?

In 1534 the French explorer Jacques Cartier sailed into the Gulf of St. Lawrence in what is now Canada. He claimed the land there for his country, and the region became known as New France.

Who followed in the explorers' footsteps?

Settlers did. In November 1620, for instance, a ship called the *Mayflower* sailed into what is now Cape Cod Bay, Massachusetts. On board were 102 English settlers, or immigrants, who became known as the Pilgrims.

● The *Mayflower's* crew nicknamed the settlers "puke-stockings" because they were so seasick during the crossing from England!

Who blazed a trail across the Rockies?

North America is a huge continent, and almost 200 years passed before explorers found their way along its rushing rivers and across its mighty Rocky Mountains to stand on the eastern shore of the Pacific Ocean. The trailblazers were Meriwether Lewis and William Clark in November 1805.

● Lewis and Clark were helped by a Shonone Native American woman named Sacagawea, who acted as their interpreter.

How did the Pacific Ocean get its name?

PACIFIC OCEAN

The first explorer to find a route around the Americas was Ferdinand Magellan from Portugal. In 1519 he set sail from Spain and went south into the Atlantic Ocean. He passed the tip of South America just over one year later. Because the ocean on the continent's far side was calmer than the Atlantic Ocean, Magellan named it the Pacific, meaning "peaceful."

● Sailing across the Pacific Ocean took much longer than expected. Magellan's men ran out of food and had to eat rats, leather, and even sawdust!

● Magellan set out from Spain with five ships and around 240 men. Only three ships made it to the Pacific Ocean.

Who first sailed around the world?

Magellan's expedition was the first to complete this amazing feat, but only one ship and 18 men made it safely home to Spain in 1522. Sadly Magellan himself wasn't on board with them—he was killed by local people in the Philippine Islands in 1521.

What is the Northwest Passage?

It's a sea route around the top of North America that was discovered in the 1840s by British explorer John Franklin. Tragically he and his crew didn't make it all the way through the passage—they died after their ships got stuck in the ice.

Why is Doctor Livingstone famous?

In the 1850s the Scottish explorer Doctor David Livingstone became the first European to cross Africa from west to east. His amazing three-year journey helped make him a legend back home in Great Britain.

Who cracked the puzzle of the longest river?

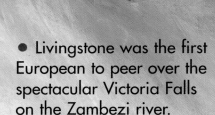

● Livingstone was the first European to peer over the spectacular Victoria Falls on the Zambezi river.

Until the 1860s Europeans had no idea where the Nile, the world's longest river, began. Then British explorer John Hanning Speke proved that it flowed out of the vast African lake that is today known as Lake Victoria.

● In 1864 Florence White Baker and her husband Samuel became the first Europeans to see the huge lake that is now called Lake Albert.

Why did some explorers wear dresses?

Women explorers always wore dresses! Although most 19th-century explorers were men, a few brave women also set out to carve a path into the unknown. They included British explorer Mary Kingsley. In the 1890s she put the comforts of home behind her and traveled all the way to Africa to study its people and its wildlife.

● Mary Kingsley was the first European woman to climb Mount Cameroon, one of Africa's highest mountains.

Who named the kangaroo?

In 1770 British explorer Captain James Cook became the first European to land on Australia's east coast. No one is certain what the native aborigines called their country's unusual hopping animals—but Cook and his men believed the aboriginal word was "kangaroo."

When did Europeans discover surfing?

Captain Cook and his men were the first Europeans to see anyone surfing in 1769. The surfers were natives of the Pacific island of Tahiti.

● In 1642 Dutchman Abel Tasman became the first European to visit the island off Australia's southeast tip. Today it is still called Tasmania.

TASMANIA

● On their long voyage, not one of Cook's men suffered from scurvy—a killer disease caused by lack of vitamin C. This was due to their special diet, which included orange and lemon juice and pickled cabbage!

Which explorers crossed Australia?

In February 1861 Robert Burke and William Wills became the first European-born explorers to cross Australia from south to north. It took them almost six months to complete their mammoth 1,860 mile (3,000km) trek across the heart of the continent.

● Burke and Wills had two companions, Charles Gray and John King. Only King made it home again—the other three all died of hunger in the outback.

When did the Beagle set sail?

A ship called the *Beagle* carried a British scientific expedition around the world in the 1830s. Exploration then was as much about discovering new plants and animals as it was about finding new places.

- One of the *Beagle's* scientists' most amazing finds was the four-foot (1.2-m)-long giant tortoise of the Galapagos Islands.

- The *Beagle's* most famous crew member was scientist Charles Darwin.

Why were some explorers also artists?

Before the camera was invented the only way to record things was to draw or paint them. Artists were key team members on the early voyages of scientific exploration.

Which explorers dived the deepest?

In January 1960 Jacques Piccard of Switzerland and Don Walsh of the United States became the first ever people to dive to the world's deepest place—the bottom of the Marianas Trench, 6.8 miles (11km) below the surface of the Pacific Ocean.

Are there chimneys under the sea?

Since the 1960s scientists have made all types of astonishing underwater discoveries—including chimneylike structures that gush smoke-colored water up from underneath the seabed!

Which explorers were the first to the North Pole?

Two Americans claimed this record—Frederick Cook in 1908 and Robert Peary in 1909. No one is sure whether either man actually made it to the pole, but most people think that Peary's claim is the strongest.

● Peary didn't do it alone—he took along his friend Matthew Henson and a four-man team of Inuit.

Who won the race to the South Pole?

In 1911 two teams led by Norwegian explorer Roald Amundsen and Briton Robert Scott battled to be the first to the South Pole. The winners were Amundsen's men on December 14, 1911. Their 800 mile (1,300km) trek across the polar ice had taken 56 days.

● Scott's team finally made it to the South Pole on January 17, 1912. Sadly all five men died of cold and hunger on their return journey.

What is a polar explorer's best friend?

A strong husky dog is excellent at battling the bitter weather of polar regions. Huskies helped give Amundsen's team the winning edge. The Norwegians used 52 dogs to pull the sleds carrying their tents, food, and other supplies.

● The British team tried to use ponies to pull their sleds. Unfortunately they weren't up to the job, and Scott's men ended up hauling their own sleds.

Who were the first people in space?

Yuri Gagarin

Russian Yuri Gagarin was the first person ever to travel into space in April 1961.

- The first animal in space was a dog named Laika in 1957.

The first woman to get liftoff was Russian Valentina Tereshkova in June 1963.

Valentina Tereshkova

When were the Moon landings?

The first people ever to walk on another world were Americans Neil Armstrong and Buzz Aldrin. Their landing craft touched down on the Moon's surface in July 1969.

Is there anywhere left to explore?

We still have a lot to learn about our planet. There are many hidden mysteries in the oceans' depths and at the frozen poles. But the biggest unsolved mysteries lie beyond Earth—space is the final frontier for modern-day explorers!

● It's expensive and dangerous to send people into space, so robots are used instead. Since 1997, for instance, three tiny robot rovers have landed on Mars and explored its surface.

● The Cassini-Huygens mission reached the beautiful planet of Saturn in July 2004. Robot probes studying its rings of ice and its moons may unlock many of the mysteries of our own planet's history.

Index